Memories, Past and Present

Ron Palmer

authorHOUSE®

AuthorHouse™
1663 Liberty Drive
Bloomington, IN 47403
www.authorhouse.com
Phone: 1-800-839-8640

First published by AuthorHouse 5/4/2011

ISBN: 978-1-4567-6158-5 (ebk)
ISBN: 978-1-4567-6157-8 (sc)

Library of Congress Control Number: 2011906969

Printed in the United States of America

THE STIMULUS

We are in a recession in case you didn't know,
But those in congress say that the economy is slow.
The President has a solution he created just for us,
it's what he likes to brag about it's called a stimulus.

There is a stimulus to put us in the mood for
Buying things, and then there's one for floods
For tornados, earth quakes, and hurricanes.

A stimulus for helping banks,
with mortgages, and cars,
another for those in higher seats,
for Restaurants and bars.

A stimulus for oil spills,
and one to save fish and birds,
I bet there might even be,
A stimulus for words.

A stimulus for fighting wars in Iraq and
Pakistan, now one up on boarders, our
Neighbor the Mexican.
I wonder what would happen if I should
Die from all the fuss.
If my family could cry and shout to get a Stimulus.

FORGIVING

Yesterday I read of a mother,
who died overdosed on drugs,
perhaps she was but one of many,
swept under societies rugs.

She left behind her a family,
what was she thinking of,
She had a husband and children,
Who only just needed her love.

The children she nourished at birthing,
A husband she once did admire,
all lost In the throws of oppression,
Given up for a newfound desire.

I wonder if she would have listened,
If someone would have tried to explain,
That every one suffers from problems In life,
but they don't throw their lives down the drain.

They don't leave behind hearts to be,
Broken, or children in need of the hugs,
For they fought back the depression,
And stayed away from the carnage of drugs.

I pray that she be forgiven,
as she crosses that spiritual line,
For God and he only can forgive her,
For the misery that she left behind.

Ron Palmer

ABOUT ME

The infant in me did nothing but cry,
And the toddler was always overly shy,
The teen was often beat down and abused,
While the young man appeared to be always confused.

The middle aged me was trying to change,
While the elder was surveying his life,
But all they could do is look back in vain,
To the years of the pain and the strife.

I know that there must have been lessons
To learn, somewhere back in the past,
But I was challenged to every turn,
By the things that I couldn't grasp.

I pray that when life has ended,
God will take this wretched man,
And change him to what was intended,
That he might fit to Gods plan.

LEARNING

At night I punch into my HP: PC.,
I light up my monitor and tap me a key,
Head to the net to see what may be,
hook up to the link with poetry.

There I log into the better or best,
writers who quickly put me to test.
To see if I have rhythm or rhyme,
or whether I'm one of those wasting my time.

Challenging me to see what I know,
and whether or not I am writing pro quo,
They really take pride in correcting my flaws,
and sometimes take effort to give me applause.

My critiques painstakingly peer at the screen,
to see if I'm writing absurd or serene,
I know I'm not Shakespeare nor am I unique,
to be a good poet is all that I seek.

And if they're persistent in playing their role,
they'll find me at least halfway in reaching my goal.

Ron Palmer

LIFE

What would you have in this life if you could,
A chance to be bad, a choice to be good,
A door to all wealth,
or would you rather have health.

Would you reason it out with logical thought,
Or just go through life with whatever you've got.

Life gives you back what you put out you know,
It's that way no matter where you might go,
If you wish to be great, step up to the plate,
For most things are lost when you hesitate.

The question is answered,
If you search really good,
What would you have in this life,
if only you could.

CANCER

There is a darkness in my life even though I face the sun,
For some vile thing has crept into my system there to run.

I did not see it coming and I am most assured,
It came to me in secret, unfelt and quite unheard.

As it eats within my body an insidious kind of blight,
Stealing my existence filling up my brain with fright.

Holding me in bondage tethered as a slave might be,
Only God could intervene and set my body free.

So I will pray unceasing into every blessed night,
until this prey has left me, turning darkness into light!

Ron Palmer

THE NEXT TIME

I fired up the ole computer,
Double clicked a page or two,
Read a message on the screen,
That said hello! And how are you.

Well then she said I was just browsing,
And I came across your name,
At a poetry connection,
With a poem of yours in frame.

Then she said I saw your email,
So I thought I'd drop a line,
To let you know my feelings,
That your poetry is fine.

Seemed to easy I was thinking,
Just to type some words and send,
And suddenly there on the net,
I found myself a friend.

I was right it was too easy,
She's gone, but she was discrete,
The next time someone writes me
I will just click on delete.

PRIDE

A proud spirit lies within a vain heart,
Circumspect to all it does impart.

Not gainfully adepted to the truth,
And sometimes tends to be a bit uncouth.

Unwary of the victims of it's pride,
Nor to the vanity it must abide.

Imprisoned by uncertainty of its days,
There by changing nothing of its ways.

Finding then the only truth it can,
That pride doth goeth before the man.

I BELIEVE

I believe in the inspiration,
Of the word both old and new.
The creation of man by an act of God,
The birth of me and you.

The virgin birth of the son of God,
Jesus Christ by name.
Who came to rid the world of hate,
Ridicule and shame.

And though we did not share his cross,
Might in our hearts least grieve the loss.
For he shed his blood so graciously,
That we might live eternally.

THE STORM

A voice cries out in the midst of the night,
Momma, momma, I'm scared,
You reply, yes honey I know,
It's only God breaking up the clouds,
So he can make the flowers grow.

But momma, why is he making so much noise,
And why is the noise so loud,
does he have to do more work,
To break a bigger cloud.

Momma what is that flash,
It's such a bright light is it good or bad,
Well that's so he can see his work at night,
you know just like your dad.

Will he be working all night,
I hope the rain doesn't get too deep,
Yes he'll be busy for a while,
It will be alright honey, now go on back to sleep.

Ron Palmer

APOCALYPTIC VIEW

I heard children crying, saw people dying,
and old ones bowed their heads,
women praying and some were saying,
that they couldn't count the dead.

Missiles flying, buildings crushed,
And politicians breaking trust,
Devastation of creation a world,
Surely torn asunder.

I saw this and much, much, more,
In hatred bitter plunder,
One wonders why it happened,
Loss of so many lives,
And yet we know it will go on,
As long as man survives.

And if he doesn't make a change,
Or take it for what it's worth.
There'll be nothing left to save,
Of this most precious earth.

THE DREAM

In days like these an inspiration,
Is not easy for us to come by,
For the young and old, and in between,
The heroes have all said goodbye.

Those on the screen,
In the days that were lean,
Have drifted into thin air,
And all that's left is a memory,
Caught up in a world of despair.

Still we cling to the right,
To believe in these things,
For that is the heart of esteem,
As the hope that we share,
By the few that still care,
Is fueled by the vision, the dream.

Ron Palmer

FROM MEMORY

From memory I can recall a little boy,
Who always seemed so sad,
One never knew in those times,
That the world could be so bad.

But no one walked in his shoes,
Felt the anguish, or the pain,
Never heard his crying in the night,
Or the prayers all said in vain.

Folks said it wasn't all that bad,
Said he could make it if he'd try,
But he worked hard throughout his life,
And the good times passed him by.

What happened to the dreams he had,
The visions put in store,
He like many others,
Failed from being poor.

Poor in spirit poor in health,
Lacking love, and lacking wealth,
Brought down by someone else's dreams,
A loss of hope to him it seems.

Yet he went on, but just as well,
The world would never know his hell,
For he was willing still to give,
No love for life, but glad to live.

A DAY IN INFAMY

Washington, New York, Pennsylvania, have a common thread today,
for they were all molested by, strangers from far away,
they came in a cowardly fashion to cause this great devastation,
given to reason by their leaders that they were just cleansing a nation.

We were made to watch in horror,
as some fell or jumped to their death,
while others suffered the agony,
as planes belched their fiery breath.

The devil did surely embrace us,
as the buildings collapsed to the ground,
while debris fell over observers,
who were screaming and running around.

Even now as the dust starts to settle,
there are those who search for the dead,
while others stand by in mourning,
drenched by the tears they have shed.

Still others are voicing their hatred,
for this terrible thing that's been done,
a new day to live in infamy,
to be known as the day 9-11

Ron Palmer

FEARS

I've lost many friends and loved ones,
In my life along the way,
And many times thought to myself,
That very soon would be my day.

I shall not go into it willing,
For I fear that vast unknown,
Because of roads that I have taken,
Seeds of misery that I've sown!

God knows I've had some good intentions,
And at times felt much depraved,
He also said these things were which,
The road to hell was paved.

Should I cry out in darkest hours!
Facing him, just alone,
I wonder if he'll even listen,
That save through prayer, I might atone.

I only know with hope in hope,
I pray he'll give me faith anew,
That when he beckons me in calling,
His love alone will see me through.

THESE HANDS

These hands were once so very strong
These hands of mine you see.
For they were put to strenuous tasks
By those who ruled of me.

I did not rale or prattle
Nor speak about my woe,
I knew that one day I'd grow old
They'd have to let me go.

And age I did as years went by
My hands became more strong,
I knew that soon they'd let me go
To keep me would be wrong.

They let me go, and life's demands
Called out for need of stronger hands,
But I in bitter past recalling
Denied the call for new commands.

The years have come and the years have gone,
And now I'm faced with family plans,
Requiring of me to still be strong
But pleading of me to have tender hands.

MY GIRLS

If I should fail to say goodbye,
To my precious, precious, girls,
Thinking to remember them in braces
Pony tails and curls.

If I should miss those open smiles
Or see them before I leave,
I hope they will forgive me
I pray they do not grieve.

They were the best of their mom
And I the best that they would be,
No one could ever be more proud as
We were of all three.

So if I should fail to say goodbye
To my precious, precious, girls all three,
I pray that they will remember at the least,
Something good about me.

LOOKING BACK

Today I ponder over life,
Things I did or didn't do,
And realized in thinking this
How often that I failed you.

It wasn't my intent back then,
Things just turned out that way,
I found myself not knowing,
Just what to do or say.

Now here I am so old and lame
Just looking back to then,
Wishing that I could change it all,
Now isn't that a shame.

I guess all I can do is love you till I'm gone,
And pray God bring us back together
When this life is done.

Ron Palmer

NO MIRACLE BUT LOVE

When just a millionth of a speck began to grow within the womb,
And then a movement noticed it began to need more room,
Twas said this is a miracle a sign from up above,
Indeed this was no miracle no miracle but love.

A body lay still on a bed life slowing ebbing out,
They said he's gone and then hysterically began to shout.
Then sudden as it came, death went like the fluttering of a dove,
Twas a miracle they said again a sign from up above,
But the one who lived thought to himself,
No miracle but love.

Across the sea in swamps and fields men fight some die there,
Others make it home again with loved ones lives to share.
They wonder how they got home safe to see the ones they love,
And think perhaps a miracle came from up above,
Twas indeed no miracle no Miracle but love.

No miracle but love could start the growing of a seed,
Or bring back life into a man who'd seen his death indeed.
Or answered prayers of loved ones who's men were battle worn,
And thought they'd never see again the land where they were born.

So if you speak of miracles,
know what your speaking of,
There's only one that will be true,
The miracle of love.

PEACE

The news that day was tragic
And very hard to bare,
How could someone be so evil,
How could they just not care.

And as the day went on
The news became more wild
It broke the hearts of many
Every man and child.

Children were put to bed that night
Too afraid to close their eyes
And said a prayer with mournful cries,
Looking up at empty skies.

Dear Lord as I lay down to sleep
For brothers and sisters I do weep
And pray you watch them each night
To keep us safe within your might.

And as I do not know my fate
I ask you Lord to quench my hate
Give me a strength that will not cease
Until this world has found its peace.

Ron Palmer

THE EGO TRIP

Some folks just aren't happy
With all that they've been given,
For they are very vain inside
And by their ego driven.

They're even taking time to
Change the color of their hair
But me I'll keep just what I've got
At least I've got it there.

They complain about everything,
Even the size of their shoe's,
They just aren't happy with anything
But they haven't heard the news.

You may look the best you can,
And carry your vain pride,
But it still won't help you not one bit,
For beauty is deep inside.

No matter what you try to change
There'll always be another,
And like that old, old saying,
You can't judge a book by it's over.

NAGGING

I have nagging children,
And I have a nagging man,
They nag about most anything,
And every, thing they can.

I just can't seem to get things right,
No matter what I do,
I face their nagging from morn to night,
Until each day is through.

They nag about the things they eat,
They nag about what they wear,
It seems no matter how hard I try,
They just don't seem to care.

I don't quite know just what to do,
To change this trend of theirs,
So I guess I'll just start nagging too,
To see what fruit it bares!

Maybe they'll get tired of me,
If I start to nagging,
Perhaps it might just shut their mouths,
And keep their tongues from wagging.

Ron Palmer

MARIA WHEN YOU WERE BORN

When you were born
No one was as proud to see,
For finally something in this
World was a part of me.

The beam in my eye,
Must have been very bright
For they said I had a glow
As though bathed in sunlight.

You had the sweetest smile of any child,
Sometimes I thought you were a bit to wild.
You grew so quickly, I felt So old.
And was saddened when you left the fold.

Yet still as these things have to be,
In my heart you'll always be a part of me.
And no matter where you go or what you do,
I'll always carry a love that's just for you.

RHONDA JEAN

It seems that only yesterday,
You were daddy's little girl.
You were a quiet one so sweet,
And precious as a pearl.

A little smile that warmed,
My heart as I watched you grow,
and the memory still touches me,
and I feel a special glow.

When I hear your voice long distance,
it makes me feels so sad,
For I know that there were times,
when life just seemed so bad.

I worry about you but that's part of life,
as days and years unfold,
Here in my heart you'll always be,
your daddy's little girl.

Ron Palmer

WHISPERS

Whispers in the darkness,
of all the years gone by,
Telling of a love we had,
when we were young and shy,
Questions still are calling,
to answer still not heard,
maybe they were just too much,
as spoken by the word.

Standing in the shadows by,
and old familiar scene,
waiting for my love to come,
as though it were a dream.

Waiting, waiting, waiting,
perhaps for just a scent,
that you might still be,
standing in that place,
from which we went.

Praying yet still crying for,
That place from way back when,
Hoping yet still waiting,
To see you once again.

THE PATH TO GLORY

If I could just enlighten one poor soul,
And put them on the path to glory.
Perhaps at this point in my life I could
Truly write a story.

It would be about the courage that it
Takes to face each day, searching for
The truth in life.

Helping others in the way, about
Forging mighty rivers, where the
Currants pull and tow, taking you
To places that you did not dare to go.

Climbing over mountains with so
Ragged a terrain, that they brought
Complete exhaustion, and ladened
You with pain.

It would be about the elements that
Challenged you with force, and help
You overcome your hatred and remorse.

And finally you entered into a valley
Of relief, broken in your spirit and
Freed of all your grief!

There is a gracious ending as we finish
Out the story, for all that you've endured
You have found the path to glory.

It is not easy asking about what or where
Or why, but surely you can make it if you
Only dare to try.

Ron Palmer

WHEN

When you in daily thought accrue
More good than you had set to do,
When you can stand with chin up high,
and hear your earthly brothers cry.

When in each day,
you strive to reach your goal,
and in your path,
there find a struggling soul.

When you did smile,
and was returned a frown,
When you did help,
and not receive a crown.

When you ran the race,
and did not win,
But still you ran,
and did not give in.

When in each day,
you've done these things you've wrought,
Then you have done much better,
Then you thought.

NIKKI

I remember how you made us laugh,
In your toddler years,
The laughter that you brought to us,
Was sometimes mixed with tears.

How you chose to stay up and play
At night when we were all asleep,
And at the break of dawn, you were
Still upon your feet.

We couldn't keep up with you on any
Given day, because you had more
Energy than anyone could say.

You scared your momma half to death
By jumping from chairs and couches,
We couldn't count the times she had
To fix your scrapes and ouches.

You've grown into a woman with quite
An intellect, a woman that your mom
And I have both come to respect.

You may have been the last to come,
In that we do not measure, for deep
Within our hearts, we count each
Of you a treasure.

A MEMORIAL DAY PRAYER

With the world so full of trouble,
Filled with confusion and dismay,
Those who once used reason,
Suddenly have lost their way.

Care for others seems forgotten,
As hatred vies for world control,
Malice and destruction are eating
At mans soul.

Lord we ask your intervention,
For at least just this one day,
So that we may pay remembrance,
To those who've passed away.

That we can take a moment
To recall a better day, when streets
And homes were safer, beneath
Trees of gentle sway.

When people could be neighbors
More willing to help and share,
Who carried compassion in their
Hearts, knew what was right or fair.

So for those who've gone before, us
Who have long since set the way,
We pray for their remembrance
On this Memorial Day.

HIS WORD

As generations turn to dust,
And generations rise,
Foundation upon foundation,
The world has grown in size.

Knowledge has increased in man,
But not through gods direction,
For man has chosen to follow satin,
In the path of self selection.

But he shall have a chance to turn,
And change his revelation,
If he'll but tune his heart, and soul,
To Gods divine creation.

For he like many other generations,
Shall fall to dust,
To rise again at judgment,
And stand before the just.

With a promise of salvation,
To all who may have heard,
Since the dawn of his creation,
Our Gods most holy word.

That he may be relinquished,
Removed from all his sinning,
Transformed into a spiritual being,
As he was from the beginning.

ALONE

When I was growing as a boy,
I had great expectations,
And as I sped towards a goal,
There were many hesitations.

Which road to take, which bridge to cross,
Which mountain should I, climb,
Which things to keep in memory,
Which things to leave behind.

There were many roads to choose from,
As I traveled thru my life,
So few years of happiness,
So many years of strife.

I was told, tough times build character,
So I kept that in mind,
Hoping that the harshness,
Of life would change in time.

It hasn't changed so greatly,
But still with what I've known,
The saddest person in the world,
Is who travels it alone.

SOUL SEARCHING

Thoughts running around like scared rabbits,
With no place to alight,
Always running, never stopping,
Like frightened creatures of the night.

Fearful that someone or something,
Might creep in, and know, me for who I am,
Hidden in this vessel, still strange to me,
Full of memories to scan.

Searching always prying,
at the depths of my own soul,
Wondering what part of me,
could make me feel the whole.

Coping, always hoping,
that before this body rots,
That I might find this wondrous being
Hidden in my thoughts.

Ron Palmer

THAT MY LOVED ONES STAY FREE

One, two, three, four,
the sound of marching feet,
Shall I cry for victory,
or will I meet defeat.

For what purpose do I fight,
for what reason do I kill,
I only know the order passed,
when ready fire at will.

Steadily I march on,
through mud, rain, and sleet,
Occasionally I gaze,
at the dead on the ground at my feet.

Somebody's son or father there,
who had finally met the end,
I ask oh God will I be next,
at which corner, at which bend,

My courage falters as I see them there,
I can feel a trembling inside,
The decision is mine to make now,
As to whether to stand or hide.

The answer comes quite clearly
As I hear the trumpets call,
My country learned one thing from birth,
For one, and one for all.

One, two, three, four,
Marching, marching on,
The sound of cannons at my side,
As night, gives way to dawn.

Cont.

All thought has finally left my mind,
I've only one to save,
And that, is to remember,
I was born in the land of the brave.

That I must go on with the battle,
No matter how weary I be,
For my purpose is a little clearer now,
To see that my loved ones stay free.

To see that my country may never have,
The fear of a dictator's gun,
For this reason, and this one alone,
I will fight till the battle is won.

Ron Palmer

CRAPAW

My grandson calls me crapaw,
Don't even ask me why,
I truly think it's funny,
And I take it all in stride.

He's such a frisky little guy,
And from morning until night,
It's crapaw this and crapaw that,
Till he's in bed and out of sight.

Now I have to tell you, I don't mind,
That he calls me by this name,
For like my other grandson's,
He loves me just the same.

And I know that I'd be sad,
If he wasn't there at all,
To call me by any name,
Especially crapaw.

WHATS WRONG WITH THIS PICTURE

Everything is fine in the U.S of A,
While people are starving just a continent away.
The poor get poorer, and the rich get richer,
Pray tell me what's wrong with this picture.

I hear the people on the T.V. screen,
Speak of the horrible things that they've seen.
They fuss and argue about the color of skin,
And say gay is ok, that it's not a sin.

The homeless are lying in streets, and in pastures,
While the world is plagued with El Nino disasters.
Politicians are shouting that they're doing their best,
As they sell high tech weapons to the east and the rest.

The children are killing, and the old folks are dying,
And God up in heaven is probably crying.
As he looks down upon this unholy mixture,
And is asking, himself what's wrong with this picture.

SOFT TOUCH

Today a little hand reached out,
To touch me gently,
And to ask an age old question,
Grandpa do you love me.

To answer such a question,
Is so easy to impart,
Why sure I love you darling,
From the bottom of my heart.

Why no one means so much to me,
My little precious one,
For you make my every day seem bright,
Just like that good old sun.

And I thank you just for asking,
For it lets me know you care,
That grandpa has these feelings,
That he's more than glad to share.

So don't you fret my little one,
For what I say is true,
There'll always be a special place,
In grandpas heart for you.

OBSTACLES

When life delves out its many pains,
Placing obstacles in my path,
I do the best I can,
To control my fire, my wrath.

For God has told me, he will be,
My shield, and comfort still,
That he will guide me ever gently,
Up each steep, and craggy hill.

And should I falter, slip, or fall,
Or should I lose my way,
He tells that I merely need,
To stop right there and pray.

For even in the darkest moments,
In my greatest hour of grief,
He will touch my very being,
And give to me relief.

So I will not be wavered,
By what others tend to do,
For God has given promise,
That he will see me through.

Ron Palmer

ALL I HAVE

Lord all I have is by you given,
No goal have I but by you driven,
No heights I see but by you lifted,
All talents known are by you gifted.

Else wise I have not one small thing,
Except by mercy you did bring,
And laid it at my table bare,
To show me lord that you did care.

When in human weakness I did fail,
You came and urged me to prevail,
You said to love all people here,
That only hate could nurture fear.

You told me to keep faith in prayer,
That in dark times you would be there,
These things I know as sure as living,
That all I have is by you given.

SATAN

Before time as we know it,
Before the order of man,
He the image of greatness,
Caused a change in the plan.

Awesome in stature and powerfully adorned,
The most Handsomest creature God ever formed,
Decided that he should be master of all,
So he started a war in celestial hall.

Soon learned it was more than he could embrace,
Was thrown out of heaven in total disgrace,
And being outraged at the thought of displace,
Began the deceiving of Gods human race.

Setting out to destroy the earth and all in it,
In the end shall be thrown in the bottomless pit,
And all those who follow him in his dire mission,
Shall also follow him to perdition.

Ron Palmer

WHEN YOU BELIEVE

When you believe and others doubt you,
Because of your belief, and what you think is true,
Still you go on in what your, thinking,
Knowing what it is that you must do.

They will make a mockery of your, vision,
For they in hatred only deal in lies,
In greed and jealousy they taunt you,
Perhaps because they know you're wise.

But you will choose the dream your, after,
Knowing full well that it is a dream,
And yet it's possible for you to see it,
As the mighty ocean was spawned from just a stream.

If you can hear the truth in what's been spoken,
While others tear the truth to shreds,
The good in life through you cannot be broken,
But rather strengthened by your soul with a common thread.

When you can force yourself to keep on running,
The race is over and you did not win,
And though lost you are willing to run again,
Even though in doing so caused you pain.

When you can take a look around you,
And keep your faith in light of what you see,
Then hold your head up high and do not doubt it,
You are in the place my friend you want to be.

WORTH

Just look at you,
you seem to think that life's so bad,
One day you say your' bored,
the next day you seem so sad.

Poor little you, in your existence,
you haven't even gone the distance,
what will you do when things get hard,
It would be my guess you'll fall apart.

No will to live,
no grit or drive,
no point or goal,
for which to strive.

One day you'll find it if you should choose,
God, made no soul that he should lose,
and every man upon this earth,
should he gain knowledge shall his know worth.

Ron Palmer

THE TRUTH

The truth has been tried a found wanton,
The lie has been tried and set free,
In a society of people,
Who will blame anyone they can see.

Justice has gone thru a time lapse,
Hidden in a time long ago,
Lost on the break of a shoreline,
Along with the truth as we know.

Somewhere the system has failed us,
As counselors vie for the prize,
And only for that almighty dollar,
Will your representation be wise.

But the truth is returning I tell you,
And in its return will prevail,
While those who abide in its coming,
Will also take part the assail.

PILGRIMS

I have been on a journey,
all my life to find my quest,
I know now being fully grown,
that it has been a test.

I do not know my mission,
but perhaps I'll find out soon,
I only pray it be a good one,
and not one filled with gloom.

For I am just a pilgrim,
like all other pilgrims here,
Looking for that ray of light,
that will take away my fears.

Praying I will stand,
before the father and the son
That they will say you are finished here,
my child your job is done.

Ron Palmer

NIGHT AND DAY

Night lifts its blanket of moon and stars,
And trades it in for sunlit hours,
Where light spreads warmly ore' the meadows and glens,
Vastly amplified of heavens lens.

Displaying flowers,
gloriously arranged and all,
as though dressed up,
meet or ball.

Rivers glistening, sparkling yet,
meet others rivers without fret,
While animals forage around for food,
To kill the hunger and feed their brood.

Man busies himself in daylight hours,
Building bridges, roads, homes, and towers,
Highway bustling with trucks and cars,
Until nights blanket of moon and stars.

ALL GROWN UP

Today I sat and remembered,
Of when you were a child,
And things came through so clearly,
As my thoughts were all compiled.

I thought of all the times,
I lay you quietly to rest,
While angels hovered over you,
Each night at my request.

The years crept by so silently,
Soon you would be in school,
Learning how to deal with life,
And to live by every rule.

Suddenly you were a teen,
Who thought you knew it all,
No one could tell you anything,
As best I can recall.

Now here we are it came so fast,
And you are all grown up at last,
The time has come to say good-bye,
I promise that I would not cry.

Now you must travel on your own,
Just you to brave the world alone,
At first you'll travel by yourself,
And then you'll join somebody else.

I'll pray that you might have the best,
While angels watch at my request,
Now I'm the one who is alone,
But I'm so proud that you are grown.

I WONDER

I wonder how our world would be,
without you in it,
You who labored those long months,
right down to that very last minute.

One who clothed and fed us,
also putting us down to sleep,
It was you in worried times of sickness,
And you who took the time to weep.

You asked no recompense,
for things given to our need,
And even chastised sometimes,
for our every word or deed.

I wonder where I'd be,
if you had set us in the world no net for safety,
or stood your ground to hold us back,
whenever we were hasty.

Who all these years,
stood solemnly behind the ranks,
And calmed us through the stormy times,
with little thanks.

Today we'd like to do something,
that we don't often do,
And that is to thank God in heaven,
For a mother just like you.

A GREATER PEACE

I cannot take away your pain,
Although I wish I could,
I cannot replace your losses,
Though God knows I would.

I cannot take away your fears,
Because I have them too,
Nor can I replace what's missing,
Deep inside of you.

But I can pray to God,
To ease your sorrow,
To give to you a better day,
And an even greater tomorrow.

And I can ask him,
to do what is just,
To bring revenge to those,
Who broke your trust.

But most of all I pray that,
He'll not cease,
In bringing to this world
A greater peace.

KEEP IT SWEET

The New Year today came in with a ring,
What type of mystery do you wish it will bring,
Possibly good things for all of my friends,
Maybe a new song that we can all sing.

Perhaps a new job with much better pay,
A new bike, a new car, a new beginning today,

How will you handle this New Year you're living,
Will you use it wisely with what you've been given,
Or will you waste it today like so many do,
And go out and steal till the law catches you.

I hope you do good with what you receive,
And keep your sights on what you believe,
Just be adventurous to all you might meet,
Life goes very quickly so just keep it sweet.

REMINISCING

Today I was just sitting here reminiscing about days gone by,
Days when I would stupidly give anything a try,
Although I didn't get to high for fear of heights,
Nor to enclosed like in a fog, as I was claustrophobic.

There were days of chasing trains,
though we weren't always on the tracks,
And hopping down the sidewalks,
purposely missing all the cracks.

Of running barefoot in the snow,
on blustery winter days,
And doing other crazy things,
because it was the craze.

Many seasons have passed since then,
seasons we will miss,
Now all that's left is our memories,
While we sit and reminisce.

SWEET BABY GIRL

I've got a visitor coming soon,
Could be April, May, or June,
A sweet baby girl with big brown eyes,
Or blue, or green, when she arrives.

A heart of gold and skin so fair,
A smile that only an angel could wear,
I made plans for both she and I,
As time in this life seems to fly.

There'll be tea cup parties, a great sensation,
Birthday parties and graduation,
All these things will be a blast,
We must enjoy since life goes fast.

I don't want to miss a single thing,
That this little visitor will bring,
A prayer for her to God above,
With kisses, and hugs, and lots of love.

I've been waiting,
can't happen too soon,
Perhaps she'll be here,
in April, May, or June.

NEVER TO BIG

One day I was riding my bike down the road,
When up beside me pulled a full load.
He had oversized tires, and rims made of wires,
And a frame that seemed made for the track,
Two pipes made of solid chrome,
That stood high up in the back.

Well this joker took off, left me sitting,
Two streams of black smoke blocked my view,
I thought he's asking for trouble,
He's going to get his just due.

Then all of a sudden a grin crossed his face,
As a small cycle came into sight,
Get him little man I said,
Shut him down I said in despite.

They sat there and revved up their engines,
For a drag the hog thought a cinch,
But when the smoke had cleared away,
The hog hadn't budged an inch.

And way down the road sat the smallest cycle,
Popping and racking his pipes,
While the big man sat with an empty tank,
And twenty thousand gripes.

Well the moral to this story is clear,
If you think you're too big to be whipped,
It isn't always how big you are,
It's how well you're equipped.

Let wisdom be known if you will,
Take the best advice you can get,
Size isn't what always takes the prize,
But what's commonly known as wit.

Ron Palmer

A STUDENT

I am a student,
I come to school to learn,
This means that I must concentrate,
On what my grades will earn.

I will not judge my classmates,
By the color of their skin,
Nor by the facts of their beliefs,
For we're all human kin.

I'll do my best to keep the peace,
At this school that I attend,
And promise to treat everyone,
Who comes here as a friend.

I hope to master all that I survey,
Perhaps then to be prudent,
For after all that's why I come to school,
Because I am a student.

MOM

When I was just a babe in arms,
You held me close to you,
To shelter me from childish fears,
Because I was so new.

And when you'd lay me down to sleep,
Just so you wouldn't hear my cries,
You'd sing a sweet soft song to me,
Until I closed my little eyes.

You bandaged all my bruises,
And wiped away the tears,
And hugged away the pains of life,
Up through my growing years.

You were my source of comfort then,
An up lift to my soul,
And showed me how to be a man,
In searching for a goal.

So mom I feel that you should know,
The importance that you played,
In raising me to be a man,
Assured and unafraid.

And though my life accomplishments,
Have been but just a few,
The greatest thing I have of all,
Is the love I have for you.

Ron Palmer

THE BULLY

This is a story,
of a boy I once knew,
If you read this,
perhaps it will give you a clue.

He was always hitting and pushing,
gouging and shoving his peers,
Whatever it took,
till he brought them to tears.

For him,
this was an everyday thing,
And as bullies go,
he thought he was king.

He'd walk down the halls,
of the school everyday,
searching for the weakest kids,
Searching, for his prey.

It wasn't wrong from his thoughts,
He did derive,
For his father had told him,
only the strong will survive.

So he in the wake,
of his father's great claim,
Set out to prove what he did,
With no shame.

Until one day at the end of his quest,
Another bully put a knife in his chest,
The moral of the story is this, if you may,
Live your life by violence and you'll die the same way.

JACOBS MIND

God has a bit of humor,
I can see that this is true,
I have a roommate Mr. Bright,
Who's short a bulb or two.

He is a friendly sort of bloke,
Who's brawn makes up for brain,
And you don't want to make him mad,
He could inflict some pain.

Now Jacob helps the people out,
Here at the nursing home,
That is because he likes to work,
And because he feels alone.

He collects all kinds of things,
From clocks to fishing poles,
From hoards of socks and racing cards,
To pictures that please the soul.

The stories that he talks about,
In days when he was young,
Are conjured up to be half truths,
About things he'd wished he'd done.

It's true these things in Jacobs mind,
For his mind it tends to roam,
to see great visions in his thoughts,
to find himself a home.

LETTER FROM A SOLDIER GIRL

Dear momma,
Day 1
I thought I'd send you this letter to let you know,
That we arrived safely in Iraq,
While we get settled in, I thought I'd send you the
Address so you could write me back.
I want you and dad to know that I'll do my best,
To do you proud,
I remember you saying don't hang with the wrong crowd.
I've been listening to some of the men they say
A women's place is home cooking,
and taking care of children.
It seems I read somewhere that the female of any
Species could and would be more aggressive at
Defending their young than any male.

Day 2
Momma, today we ran into an Iraqi unit we had
Fierce fight several on each side were hit.
Truthfully I was more in fear of those behind me
Than those in front.
It's bad enough to be worried about the enemy
When friendly fire is where you get the brunt.

Day 3
Well momma we made it through the night I
Guess I'm lucky I didn't get hit by either side.
I did get some rude remarks from a few men
That I considered bad, but I just thought to myself
They don't make men any more like dad.
I'd probably get a more warmer response if I
Were captured by Iraq.
Who then supposedly those two would watch my back.
Well momma, I guess I'll close for now,
Try not to worry I'll try not to falter, keep safe
Keep well.
Love always your daughter.

LETTER FROM A SOLDIER BOY

Dear mama, today we're going to fight,
in an unfamiliar place,
our sergeant says don't worry,
He says just keep up with the pace.

I can see it on the faces,
of the men beside me here,
What I feel deep down inside myself,
and that feeling would be of fear.

Our lieutenant says keep moving,
we are nearing our next phase,
And if we do good we'll be out of here,
in just a few more days.

Well mama night has fallen,
and you are in my prayers,
by the way I am able to write,
Using the light from flares.

Sorry ma I must stop now,
as the enemy he is near,
And I must concentrate,
on everything I see and hear.

My friends are watching my back,
Just as I am watching theirs,
it really works for the best,
When we are out in pairs.

I must close now ma to get this out,
Wanted to let you know I'm fine.
I'll write again when things slow down,
Hopefully I'll have a bit more time.

I'll say goodbye for now ma,
Give my love to everyone,
and as I close this letter I'll say ma,
I love you too, your son.

Ron Palmer

DECEPTION

Our country is close to anarchy and chaos in the streets,
Brought about by the economy and those in senate seats.
Promises that were not kept by those that we all know,
done in the night while we all slept in places we don't go.

Lies from the upper echelon passed down for us to see,
to make us think that it is truth but it will never be.
Freedoms that we do not have we thought we had before,
but they were lost long ago in hypocritic lore.

America is truly blind and this justice for which it stands,
has been sold to those who do not care and placed in careless hands.
We say that we believe in God yet we don't obey his word,
and every time we are approached we say we weren't heard.

It's time for us to listen before it is too late,
Or we will lose our country to those who live by hate.
To those who promise our demise and all who walk our shores,
fueled by the things that we despise brought to our very doors.

If you know a prayer then just say it and if faithfully employed,
it just may keep our country from being totally destroyed.

WHERE MEMORIES STAY

The years that we've been together
Have molded us into one,
And no other women would have taken,
All of the things that I've done.

Yet still you stood by me,
In good times and in bad,
Sharing all the joy's and the sorrows,
That we two have had.

You don't know my admiration,
For the courage that you've shown,
Nor do you know of the sadness,
Inside this man that you've known.

The sacrifices you've made,
for the kids and me,
Have filled up a place within my soul,
that you may never see.

And so here you are in my thoughts,
Every minute, every hour, every day,
And will be there as long as we live,
In a place where memories stay.

Ron Palmer

DAD

Who worked so hard to keep us straight,
Whenever we did wrong,
and sacrificed with willingness,
To push us all along.

Gave us the best of his advice,
that our thinking might be clear,
even though it seemed to him,
That we just couldn't hear.

Who gave to us unselfishly,
when he had things to give,
and tried to make us look at life,
A bit more positive.

Who faces all his trials,
as bravely as he can,
And wanted everyone he met,
to respect him as a man.

Who requires no medals or rewards,
for all he has done,
He just wants his family as a family,
to present themselves as one.

LOOKING BACK

When I was just a boy in knickers,
That were held up with a rope,
It seemed the world was somewhat gentler,
Perhaps still held a little hope.

Dream chasers flourished,
Worked their magic night and day,
Then came those who hated dreamers,
And they took their dreams away.

They never seemed to be contented,
Those others saw the bigger scheme,
To them it was an easier challenge,
To steal someone else's dream.

And so today the world is bitter,
Full of jealousy and hate,
Filled with rage and discontentment,
With no concern to change to change their fate.

Blaming others for their failures,
Lacking in their self esteem,
And only those that have the money,
Can afford to have the dream.

FLESH AND BONE

When the man is dead,
And the soul is gone,
All that's left is flesh and bone.

But the flesh was weak,
And the bone was dried,
And the soul was lost before he died.

Well he did his best when
He was alive,
The best he could to try to survive.

He took the ride to the very end,
And only then did he start to bend.

He chose to take the journey alone,
It was his wish to be on his own,
So please forgive him lord,
He tried to atone,
For after all he was flesh and bone.

But the flesh was weak,
And the bone was dried,
And his soul was lost before he died.

FRIENDS

They say if you have one friend in life,
You have more than most dear soul,
If just one person cares for you,
You have achieved a goal.

I must be very fortunate,
thank God I have a few,
For recently having faced my death,
They came and led me through.

They did not ask my stance in life,
Or to what I could afford,
They were too busy assisting me,
With loving caring accord.

They structured me in my living,
Made me forget all of my strife,
And I thank God for these dear friends,
who walked me back into life.

Ron Palmer

GOOD SHAPE

My teeth are false so I can't chew gum,
I have a bad hand so I can't play rum.
My brain is slow so they think I'm dumb,
They make fun of me when I sit and hum.

My legs are bad it's hard to walk,
I slur some words when I try to talk,
Some say I'm as thin as an old corn stalk,
And others just stand there and gawk.

Now I know this sounds a little sad,
But it isn't really quite so bad,
I had some teeth till they got knocked out,
And my brain has always been in doubt,
My legs were walked off by the state,
And the words I spoke never were so great.

So when your down and feel a dread,
just think about these things I've said,
Remember them and contemplate
If your' better than me you're in good shape.

THE HARBOR VIEW

I've seen everything to see,
from star's to mornings dew,
To see the docks where boats are tied,
where seagulls spread their wings,
I've seen a lot and yet,
my eyes cannot avoid these things.

A mystery comes from every ripple,
A thrill with every wave,
It isn't any wonder,
that my hearts become a slave.

No it isn't any wonder,
that of all things I do,
I come around and round again,
To see the harbor view.

Ron Palmer

HOPE

It was said of ancient ages,
That hope eternal springs,
And I pray God that they were right,
In this day of evil things.

For as long as there is hope,
There's room for love,
And all the good that comes thereof.

As long as there is hope,
There's room for caring,
Room for decency and sharing.

Hope is not foolish,
Nor is it that to seem,
For only there in hope,
Springs that eternal dream.

Only in hope do we dare try
To nurture,
The seed of the past to,
Lay claim to the future.

GUIDANCE

When I was young no seeming goal,
They said I was captain of my soul,
That I was master of my fate,
Directions mine to magistrate.

But when I sorely lost my aim,
They said it was I who was to blame,
For those who taught I was profound,
Vision lost and nowhere bound.

But here I am still in the race,
Not to mine but to their disgrace,
For they were quick to show their wrath,
More quickly still to close each path.

But I have greater guidance now,
My path they cannot close,
For he who stands behind me,
Has already once arose.

And I shall never lose my way,
No need to ask reprieve,
For he shall always be there,
As long as I believe.

Ron Palmer

CRITICIZE

Who am I to criticize,
About what you say or do,
Who am I to criticize,
When I am just like you.

I go about my business,
Keeping counsel to myself,
And when the day is over,
Place my glasses on the shelf.

I read the news and tend my thoughts,
Perhaps the same as you,
Then I sit back and watch TV,
See the evils that men do.

And when it's over,
And all is said,
I begin then to surmise,
And ask again to me, myself,
Who am I to criticize.

WHAT GOOD

When I was just a child,
I was much confused at best,
Dreams of happiness misfiled,
In searching for a quest.

Dormant of all challenges,
That my life could bring,
Loneliness and sadness,
Were to all that I could cling.

While others found achievement,
I found only hate,
And when they tried to show me love,
I would only tend to grate.

But one day someone told me,
What you give in life you get,
And you'll never know of happiness,
In the ways that you are set.

Now I've found another outlook,
As I face the years ahead,
Just a kind word from a stranger,
And my thoughts are better fed.

Never question good or evil,
Of the reason for them being,
If you cannot see the good in life,
Then what's the good in seeing.

ANGEL OF OUR OWN

When we were lost, directions crossed,
We prayed for angels to intervene.
Like many things they never came,
Perhaps too busy with greater things.

When aspirations met new heights,
And we needed a hand to push us through.
Jodi was the one we called,
the one who was there to lead us through.

Her persistence with us always shines,
Revealing all that good divines,
She teaches while the children learn,
The need to know each twist or turn.

Her guidance keeps the path renewed,
Through courage and her fortitude,
And now we've found what we should have known,
We've had an angel of our own.

HEROES

There's a growing need for heroes,
In this world in which we live,
Heroes of the type that never take,
But rather give.

They who speak to elders with respect,
Not degradations,
Teaching children self esteem,
And not of deprivations.

Those who help their neighbors,
When they know the need is there,
And ask not one small farthing,
Doing it just because they care.

Yes the world has need for heroes,
Not brought about by whim,
But the type of heroes who are there,
When you have need for them.

Ron Palmer

MARIA

You say that I don't love you,
You say I put you down,
And yet more times than one,
I have picked you off the ground.

Why I've bragged more times about you,
To people that I knew,
How smart I thought you were,
And how proud I was of you.

Why is it that you always seem,
To think that I don't care,
Have I not told you more than once,
How I'm glad that you've been there.

You can't seem to get the message,
And I think that this is sad,
I just want things to be better for you,
Better than I have had.

God knows I'll love you,
In good times or in bad,
And when your life starts getting better,
I'll be more than glad.

God put you in my life,
Surely you must know I care,
And I'd be a whole lot poorer,
If he hadn't put you there.

JUST TO THINK

In the quiet of the evening,
When the sun has run its course,
And the patterns of the heavens,
Change by some un-doubting force.

When the trees begin to whisper,
Put in motion by the wind,
My mind too has a motion,
From which my thoughts transcend.

And I've pondered all I've said,
Perhaps even done this day,
Wondering if I could have changed it,
Had I chose another way.

That's when my conscience tells me,
It really doesn't matter,
For when all is said and done,
We could all do so much better.

It's nice that were thinking,
That we were not contrite,
For when we stop to think and reason,
Everything will be alright.

JUST ONE SMALL PAIR OF SHOES

There's happiness within a heart,
And sadness when you lose,
But joy leaps into your heart,
In one small pair of shoes.

A child takes over all your thoughts,
And drives away your blues,
You wonder how much could come,
In one small pair of shoes.

Just one small pair of shoes,
Has jumped from nothing into life,
Making you forget you had one,
Least bit of strife.

Your, richer than you've ever been,
And you'll never get to choose,
A greater thing than that which came,
In one small pair of shoes.

FREE

When the Great Spirit, chooses,
For a warriors soul to rise,
One hears the roar of thunder,
See the eagle as he flies.

The bear stands tall as guardian,
And the wolves all gather round,
To give this warriors soul a path,
To the happy hunting ground.

The hawks cry out a message,
To the tribes both near and far,
As they look towards the heavens,
And see another flaming star.

To them new life is praise,
Of the things that are to be,
And death is just the passage way,
For the spirit to be free.

Ron Palmer

LOOKING FOR GOD

I searched for God all through my life,
It seems I could not find him,
And so I thought in finding him,
My chances might be slim.

He isn't what the hand can touch,
Or what the eye can see,
He's more than that,
He is the thoughts of tenderness in me.

He is the vastness of this world,
The moon, the stars, the sun,
The trees, the mountains, valleys and hills,
And all the seasons rolled in one.

Thunder, lighting, rain and snow,
Are, part of his attire,
Compassion, kindness, goodness, and love,
Are strengthened in his fire.

And so I've found after all this time,
And through all things I've been,
If you wish to search for God my friend,
You'll have to look within.

IN THE EYES OF GOD

Life is but a moment,
in the eyes of God,
Short and narrow is the road,
Wherein the saints have trod.

Vain is man proud and as shallow as his breath,
Deaf to truth and justice blind unto his death,
Failing in his spirit reaching out to fight,
Tearing down his future just a shadow in Gods light.

He is speechless as he kneels,
and knows not what to say,
Because of years of silence,
he's forgotten how to pray.

But God is generous to fault,
even though the road looks grim,
For he promised us a savior,
if we'd just call on him.

So if we seek the high ground,
we must not tarry,
we dare not nod,
For life is just a moment,
in the eyes of God.

Ron Palmer

FAITH

Now faith is the substance,
For things hoped for,
The evidence of things not seen.

And for this sinful body,
Grace comes to intervene.

Then God in endless mercy,
To a temple nearly wrought,
Placed his ever boundless wisdom,
In the things that he begot.

Imputing love and righteousness,
Into an empty shell,
God sanctified with spirit there,
To keep the soul from hell.

And then to seal his bond with us,
Redemption he did give,
That thru the blood of Jesus Christ,
We would eternal live.

BECAUSE HE LOVED US

Upon the cross our savior died,
our beloved surely dead.
twas not a drop but all,
of his precious blood was shed.

Why is it that an artist shows him,
with a drop or two,
when world my God oh wretched world,
he shed it all for you.

He died in agony and shame,
for all around to see,
and yet one never shows the blood,
That flowed at Calvary.

Oh Lord how little do we know,
how often do we fail,
to realize that with his blood,
we enter thru the veil.

And should we tremble slightly,
when we touch the sacred cup,
let us look towards the cross and know,
it's our Lords blood we sup.

And so beloved, in this moment,
as we in group partake,
let us do so in spirit, love and truth,
For ours and for heaven's sake.

Ron Palmer

BOUND TO WIN

I have tried and failed, and tried
And failed again,
But surely Lord if I keep trying,
I am bound to win.

Surely you will touch me Lord,
And free my soul from doubt,
And make me a better man,
A man much more devout.

A man to see the truth in life,
More able to discern,
Between good and evil in himself,
A man more apt to learn.

To help his brother face his trials,
As he bends toward the wind,
To know that he will be much stronger,
Though he tries and fails again.

That he stays in the running,
Though the road may have a bend,
If he just keeps on trying Lord,
He's surely bound to win.

POTENTIAL ENERGY

The energy God gave to man
Is all but costly spent.
That his potentiality,
Must to the grave be spent.

His source of power is all burned out,
His kilometric seeds,
Have blown about within the winds,
Of his unearthly deeds.

He has no amperage in life,
His voltage stream is thin,
And all the atoms of his mind,
Are flexible within.

All circuits of his thoughts are loose,
With his resistance bowed,
His source will all but carry him,
His soul to meet life's load.

Conductance will not help him now,
His nucleus to save,
For he has long been headed for
The great short circuit wave.

If man would wish to make it now,
It's plain as it can be he'll have to start
All over with potential energy.

23RD PSALM POEM

The Lord IS MY Shepherd,
In him I shall not want.
He in the greenest grasses,
Will place my limbs when taunt.

To calmer waters shall he lead,
And there restore my soul.
To teach me of his righteousness,
In his name make me whole.

And though I walk in timely death,
I shall not fear of ill.
For his great rod and staff, will be
My shield and comfort still.

Then he a table shall prepare,
Mine enemies to see,
Him to anoint my head with oil,
And fill my cup for me.

Goodness and mercy will follow me,
All my days to be,
And I shall dwell in the Lords house,
For all eternity.

FREE ME LORD

Oh Lord mighty and awesome in all thy ways,
To whom all righteous men do praise.

I come before thee with spirit low,
to ask thy guidance that I might know,
why thou hast turned thy face from me.

Making all my thoughts mine enemy,
for all I do I seem to fail,
my losses and my pain prevail.

I ask for mercy Lord, show me how to obtain
Forgiveness that I may grow,
to understand thy love for me,
That from thy wrath I may be free.

ALL THINGS ARE POSSIBLE

Lord I come before you humbly,
As I'm feeling somewhat worried,
For the things that plague us in this life,
Seem to press us to be hurried.

You see my daughter Lord, is ailing,
With a thing she cannot see,
And they'll be operating Lord,
To try and cut it free

So I'm asking you to be present Lord,
As the surgeon holds the knife,
And guide her ever gently,
To spare my daughter's life.

And bring her home safely,
To her three little boys,
Who have yet to experience,
All her hopes and her joys.

Please let my prayer be faithful Lord,
As I put my pen to task,
That you in mercy grant us Lord,
All that we may ask.

GREAT-GREAT GRANDMA

I've often wondered about the ripples,
When a pebble hits the water,
How far they go how many they make,
As they journey vast and free out across the lake.

And then I realize that we just like the
Ripples, bough out to endless time
Held to each other in a gentle ebbing mime,
Sometimes we change a bit

By a harsh or gentle storm
Or are we held back by a winter freeze
Yet still we ripple in and out
With every flowing breeze.

And then while looking back in awe I think
Of you great, great, grandma
And I know that I have come full circle of
Such a wondrous being and thank God
Thru you for all my heart, is seeing
And thank him too for what I know
That thru you grandma and ma
I go on in endless flow.

A MOTHERS PRAYER

Dear son: I know those walls are hard to bear,
When you think nobody cares,
but son you are the meaning,
the heart of all my prayers.

I know it's hard to understand,
when others talk and sneer,
but I couldn't persecute you,
It was I who brought you here.

I'd give my life to see you free,
before the break of dawn,
if I could see your smile once more,
before God takes me on.

And son I have more faith in you,
than anyone will know,
for tomorrow you'll be a better man,
my heart has told me so.

And son remember this,
as you go up through the years,
that mother's don't have children,
just to dry their tears.

She loves them all through life,
as a mother really should,
and even when her son goes wrong,
A mother thinks he's good.

So as I close I think of you,
as I think of no other,
and I pray that God will keep you safe,
love always your mother.

I'M SORRY

I'm sorry that my pace is slower,
When you want to take a walk,
And that my voice will sometimes
Waver when you want to talk.

I'm sorry that I can't make things,
Like I used to for you dear,
And that you sometimes say things,
That I don't seem to hear.

I'm sorry I don't tell you,
In each day just how I feel,
Even though my feelings for you are
So very real.

I guess my age has taken toll,
And given me a shove,
But until God takes my breath from me,
You'll always be my love.

LEARNING TO COUNT

My grandson said he'd like to count,
And I asked him to what amount.
So he looked up with his big grin,
And said He'd like to count to ten.

There is one spider on the wall,
And two crickets down the hall.
Three children there at play,
Four suppers on the way.

Five peas left on a plate,
Six sisters will be late.
At Seven, Dad came through the door,
Eight kids are up no more.

Nine players on TV,
Hitting balls and walking free.
Ten, oh my you sleepy head,
It's time for us to go to bed.

I like this he said with a grin,
Can we play this game again.

A PRECIOUS BOOK

There's a book that's read by many,
A book not written by pen.
Instead the author embedded it,
Deep in the hearts of men.

This book has been used for everything,
From law, to a travel guide.
And many find it a comforter,
From tears they cannot hide.

But to me this book is the only way,
Through the door of eternal life.
In which there is no bitterness,
Sorrow, pain or strife.

It's pages they unfold to me,
A story often told.
About a mansion in the sky,
With streets all paved with gold.

And the author,
has invited us to visit him someday.
In this friendly little mansion,
Just a small life span away.

But we must know the password,
When at the gate he greets us,
And if perhaps you haven't read my friend,
The word is Jesus.

Cont.

The author is the greatest even known,
For he is known as GOD,
Who framed man and breathed into,
A worthless piece of sod.

And then to save us from the wrath if hell,
His only son's life he took,
That we might reach his mansion,
Through the pages of his book.

THE CRITIC

Who are you to celebrate,
On cutting down someone's thought's,
Proclaiming to be master of the word,
Oh how I find this absurd.

You think yourself to be so great,
Because you tend to concentrate,
On finding word's that only scholars know,
How big of you, how great the show.

You put your poison quill to work,
At cutting others to the quick,
While even a child could touch the heart,
By using word's you couldn't pick.

Who are you,
Not Tennyson, Shakespeare not even a Poe,
From what offspring,
Did your conscience grow.

To what great end do you aspire,
That you could quench another's fire,
And sever all that they might think,
When hell has risen in your ink.

It's blasphemous this thing you do,
Putting all their word's askew,
To call this challenging of the art,
While tearing all they write apart.

Me, well I think that your uncouth,
Your big word's do not define the truth,
One day my friend you'll meet defeat,
With just one word and that's delete.

CHOICES

Life gives us many choices,
We decide which ones to make,
Only we are held accountable,
For the one we choose to take.

We cannot blame our neighbors,
Or our friends if we are wrong,
Only we can make decisions ,
That will keep us weak or strong.

Building bridges to our future,
To what may or may not be,
Laying highway to a better place,
Or the roads to misery.

Only time will tell the story,
Of how much we have grown,
Only we can make the choices,
That will reap what we have sewn.

THE FIRST KISS

Twas not the screeching of a hawk,
I heard with our first kiss,
But rather was a nightingale,
Whose sweet song brought us bliss.

Twas an early summer morn,
With floral odors nigh,
That we vowed to love each other,
As we stood there eye to eye.

Well many years have come and gone my dear,
But I can tell you this,
I still hear that sweet, sweet song,
That I heard with our first kiss.

Ron Palmer

THE GREAT WOLF

As the great wolf howls when the moon is in sight,
And the stars feed the darkness light,
Visions come to sleeping men,
Who when awake prophesy by them.

Believing that their dreams tell all,
They try to explain what they recall,
But they don't see what the spirit sees,
Or feel its presence in every breeze,
In everyday of every year,
Or they would hide themselves in fear.

But the great wolf knows when he howls at night,
Of all the things there in his sight,
The bear, the deer, the wolverine,
And other things that he has seen.

He knows of things that he should fear,
Especially when man is near,
For many a friend caught in a snare,
Could testify that men don't care,
But the wolf tells all in baleful tune,
When he howls at night up at the moon.

A FATHERS PRAYER

I'm sorry I wasn't prepared dear Lord,
For the call I received today,
They told me one of my children,
And her child has passed away.

Now Pozzel was only twenty one,
Her child six months old,
But I have to say when I got the call,
That it made my heart run cold.

To lose them at such an early age,
Is more than I can bare,
And I pray you take them gently,
Into your loving care.

And I pray that you will help me,
To find that grace within,
That I may one day through your love,
Be joined together with them.

ATTAINING

I cannot put faith in the dead,
For they are of past comprehension,
I cannot trust those I love or despise,
For they well define apprehension.

I must accept my despair all alone,
For these things that I cannot change,
The course of a river, the moon and the stars,
Have all been prearranged.

From the day I was born until the day of my death,
I will have made no great changes in life,
Perhaps just a small one for the better I hope,
Even though I have dealt with much strife.

I dare not care what I may become,
Or about what my future may hold,
I can only attain through a circle of friends,
What I've gained in my life until I am old.

WHAT'S IN A FACE

What's in a face,
When you look there.
A hidden glance,
A solemn glare.

A wrinkled brow,
A scar or two,
Expressionless,
A different hue.

What's in a face,
A time warped smile,
A trace of tears,
Or pain left there,
From yesteryears.

What's in a face,
Kindly reposed,
Hatred exposed,
To me what I see in a face,
Is the history of the human race.

Ron Palmer

WHO WERE THE HEROES

I've asked myself,
many times to my shame,
Who were the heroes,
Could I call them by name.

The biblical ones that I can recall,
Are Moses, Samson, David and Paul,
There were Peter, Matthew, John and King Sol,
King Solomon to the wisest of all.

There were many more heroes of that time begotten,
But over the years, have all been forgotten,
Many more too, in the last hundred years,
Who helped in the calming of our unsettled fears.

There was Ghandi, Abe Lincoln, Jonas Salk, and Einstein,
Booker T., George Washington Helen Keller who was blind,
Robert and John Kennedy, John Glenn if you please,
Martin Luther King Jr. whose voice cried for peace.

These are the men to which my thoughts befall,
These are the heroes that I can recall,
There are some today who claim to be such,
Though it seems to me they don't do very much.

They take from the poor and give the rich it all,
Claiming that they are within the rights of the law,
There are the heroes with powerful voices,
Who say they're giving us multiple choices.

When in fact by their standards,
They're not choices at all,
Yet they call themselves heroes,
Because they have the gall.

Cont.

We've had other heroes,
They're the ones we've seen,
As we've watched the movies,
projected on screen.

But they were just heroes envisioned in hope,
Virtual reality through the light of a scope,
So I ask once again and ask to my shame,
How many heroes today could you name.

Ron Palmer

WORLD GONE WILD

Churches in deception,
Politics awry,
Others shouting hatred,
To all who pass them by.

Children killing children,
We read this everyday,
Parents who were once strong,
Have somehow lost their way.

Enemies at every gate,
Spy's upon the prod,
Selling information,
To terrorists abroad.

Heading for destruction,
Exemplified by trend,
The world losing its control,
Waiting for the end.

Some on knees are praying,
For miracles to come,
While others say that GOD is dead,
Still others yet are mum.

The mysteries of the bible,
Are soon to be resolved,
Then man will know the truth of life,
And how far he has evolved.

THE ROAD TO AERODICIA

There us a place that one can go,
To cross a mythical span,
And grace a shore on distant land,
Not seen by the likes of man.

It is a sacred world a secret place,
Where darkness cannot prevail,
A place not unlike Eden,
That only the sun could pale.

A place to go,
in sorrow, pain or grief,
To find that ever enlightening,
Joy of relief.

A place to shout for victory,
To hide ones self from defeat,
No enemy could enter there,
No fear your soul could greet.

There is no greater place to go,
Your troubles to be free of,
Than the magical trip through the maze of your mind,
To the bridge of Aerodicia.

Ron Palmer

CHAINS

An old man stood on the corner,
Watching traffic come his way,
A small boy stood beside him,
Eyes showing his dismay.

The young boy asked the question,
Why is your back so bent?
The an answered somberly,
To what he thought it meant.

Son, we carry burdens all through life,
From battles lost or won,
Chains linked together, one by one,
Forged by the things we've done.

The way we treat our fellow man,
As we go from day to day,
The things we've said or done to them,
As we traveled in the way.

My chains are heavier with age,
Because I failed to learn,
And unlike you my dear sweet boy,
I failed to show concern.

I didn't seek forgiveness,
From those I did provoke,
And so my back is bent,
From the weight of my own yoke.

But I tell you now in earnest son,
be careful what you do,
Or the chains you forge in your own life,
Out of hate or discontent,
Will beg to ask the question,
Why is your back so bent?